This Book is Dedicated to Lucy, Lewis, Tenny, Andy, Josh and Nathan. We miss you and love you. You are always warm in our hearts.

TABLE OF CONTENTS

We can mistakenly believe we're prepared for certain heart-wrenching situations, yet when one actually happens, we often feel thoroughly blindsided.

Death is one of those situations. While we know, intellectually, that people in our lives—even ourselves—will die, we can be emotionally devastated when it happens.

A loved one's death uncovers so much for each of us; perhaps it reminds us of unresolved issues with the deceased, our own mortality, even the fragility of life itself. Sometimes it just plain catches us by surprise. Adding to the difficulty, in Western society we don't really have a way to deal with death. Sure, we participate in some scant rituals, but heaven help us if we talk about death too much—this heavy, morbid subject. Yet, the loss of a loved one creates so much pain that often we don't know how we'll ever survive. But we *do* survive. And we can even thrive—if we take care of ourselves through the grieving process.

I belong to a unique "club," as do several of my friends. With their loving cooperation, I wrote this book that's designed to guide people who just joined. The only membership requirement is that we've all lost siblings.

I know that, at times, the friends you'll meet in Chapter 6 had difficulty answering the questions I asked about losing their siblings. Indeed, it was hard for me to answer my own questions. I thank all of them for their candor. Because of our efforts, new "club" members might gain a better understanding of the grieving process and learn to thrive despite their huge feelings of loss.

As you read this, I assume you've just lost a sibling to death. First, let me express my deepest sympathy for your loss. No one can truly know what this means to you or assume to know how you're feeling. It's my sincere hope that this book will help you along what can only be called the rocky path of grief—a path that at times seems all too lonely and foreboding. I can tell you that after sixteen years down this path, the journey does get easier, and for the most part, the pain subsides.

It's my intention throughout this book to give you a compass to navigate the challenging path you face as a "club" member. The first chapters tell of my experience; the last one offers a variety of experiences from people of many ages; the youngest was eight when his sister died and the oldest was thirty. You'll find a wonderful range of answers to the questions asked. These answers may help you—or they may not—but I can promise you this:

When you complete this book, you'll have a better understanding of the hills and valleys you have already crossed and will still come upon on this path of grief.

Travel onward.

CHAPTER 1

THE DAY THE CALL CAME IN

IT'S A PECULIAR WAY of coding memory: We remember exactly where we were when we heard the news of certain major events in our lives. Consider, for example, where you were when you heard about the 1986 Challenger explosion. Where were you when you heard about the attacks on September 11, 2001? We talk about these two examples of major cultural events. We share in the communal shock and grief.

When I was growing up, many of my teachers and parents' friends recalled where they were when they heard President Kennedy had been shot. At the time I thought, "I don't have any shocking memory like that." Then in January 1986, the space shuttle Challenger blew up. I can tell you exactly where I was when I heard the news; sitting in chemistry class, having just learned about liquid nitrogen and its volatility.

A tragic situation can be a lot more personal—such as the notification that your sister or brother has just died. Not everyone can relate to that; a great many people simply have no idea what it's like. But those of us who've been through it know that it's a horrible, surreal experience—one that can't ever be forgotten. The way in which we deal with our loss is varied and somewhat reflective of our age at the time of loss. This book is directed at people who are at least 18. Here's my story.

I was 28 years old when my sister, Lucy, was killed on December 9, 1996. I had gone out to dinner with my girlfriend and, in a rare move, didn't bring my pager with me. After dinner, I noticed an urgent message on my pager—coded 911—and also on my answering machine. My father said to call him immediately. I did and he told me that two Boston policemen had come to the door and asked to talk to him. My mother, who answered the door, thought they were selling tickets to the Policemen's Ball and tried to get rid of them. They insisted that they needed to talk to my father, so he came downstairs. Then they told him his eldest daughter Lucy had been murdered in Chicago.

As my father unveiled this whole story, he slowly let dozens of seemingly irrelevant details unfold. I got nervous because I didn't know what he was getting at, but I could hear the grief in his voice. Still, the last thing I anticipated was that Lucy was dead. After he told me the worst, a numb feeling started at the top of my head and dropped all the way down to my toes.

Immediately, I drove to my parents' house. I had a sense that the worst possible thing had just happened to my parents and that I would have to take care of everything. (Luckily my parents were a lot more resilient than I gave them credit for.) While driving, I started a mental list of all the things that needed to be done: making funeral arrangements, going to Chicago to talk to the police and claim Lucy's body, getting her back to Boston, and so on.

After arriving at the house, I looked for my mother. She was on the phone talking to her father and stepmother. When she got off, she just looked at me and started to cry. At that moment, I saw my mother in a whole new light—as a fragile human being who felt utterly lost. I held her in my arms as she cried, feeling as if my own heart was being ripped out, seeing my mother, a person who has always been a support for me, so hurt and sad.

Next, I told my parents we had to decide a plan of action. We talked about all the things we needed to do and who would do what. Relieved, I discovered that my parents were not as incapacitated as I had imagined. It was a short meeting and we all felt better having things to do to keep our minds occupied. I spent a few more hours with them, then went home to try to sleep—without much success.

Because I couldn't sleep, I got out of bed and called friends of Lucy's and mine who lived on the West Coast. My first call was to my best friend Rick. It was his birthday and I knew he'd be out, so I left a message and told him to call me no matter what time he came in. A few hours later he did. I had to tell him about Lucy and ask him to be in Boston on

Saturday. Being my closest friend, Rick said that of course he'd be there. It was great to see him, but it still saddens me that reunions can be so happy and tragic all at once.

Then I tried to track down some of Lucy's friends—a challenge because many had married and I didn't know their married names or their husbands' names. Before long, it was daylight and time for me to go back to my parents' house and then fly to Chicago with my father. When I got to the airport, I called my manager at work to let him know I wouldn't be in for the rest of the week. I have no idea why, but I remember that I got nervous when I had to tell him. I purposely waited to phone until I knew he'd be in his office—this is just not news you'd leave on voicemail. Fortunately, our conversation went just fine. He told me to take the time I needed and asked if he could do anything to help me or my family.

We got on the plane and soon landed in Chicago, then took a taxi to the police station. There, many media representatives were actively asking questions. Clearly, this was growing into a big news story about a local murder. We walked right by them though, because they didn't know who we were or what we looked like—yet.

As we talked to the detectives, they described what they thought had happened and communicated the case as it stood. They wanted to be delicate with a particular part of the story, stating that the condition of Lucy's apartment made the collection of forensic evidence "challenging." My father said we knew that housekeeping wasn't one of Lucy's priorities. (It's a sad commentary when a person's apartment is neater after the CSI team has been through it.)

I consider myself lucky to have communicated directly with the police and gone to the scene of my sister's death. I talked in depth with the detectives about the crime at her apartment. They might have thought I was a freak, but I asked a million questions in a calm, analytical way. I must have realized this was my only chance to get my questions answered by the people who worked the case.

The fact of the matter is, we will never know what happened in Lucy's apartment. The only two people who could tell us are dead. This is one of the most frustrating parts of this experience. I wanted to know: How did what appeared to be a robbery end in murder? This and a lot of other questions will probably never be answered. I've decided that I could waste a lot of energy searching, but that having answers wouldn't make losing Lucy any easier.

Next, we went with the state's attorney to the morgue. On the way, we discussed the case and how it might be tried. I was especially concerned about how Lucy's case would be presented. I asked whether race would become an issue because the suspect in the case was African American and Lucy was Caucasian. She assured us that race wouldn't be an issue.

We also had concerns about the makeup of the jury; the population of Cook County is more than 60 percent African American and, in the aftermath of the O.J. Simpson trial, we had legitimate concerns. Again, we were assured that this wouldn't be a problem.

It was fortunate my family didn't have to go through the pain and agony of a trial as the defendant hung himself in the Cook County Prison shortly after being arrested. To say the least, this was a great relief for my family. The trial would have generated a lot of media attention and scrutiny on our family. I'm thankful that my parents didn't have to see pictures of their daughter's murdered body or hear the details of how she was killed. I'm also thankful we didn't have to endure years of trials, appeals, and possibly, the death penalty. It may sound callus or cold, but I believe that justice was served; he died the same way he killed Lucy.

At the morgue, Dad had to sign the release form for Lucy's body. I can't imagine how incredibly difficult this must have been. What parent ever imagines he or she would have to sign for their dead child's remains? The understanding staff at the morgue asked us whether we wanted to identify Lucy in person or by looking at a closed-circuit TV. Dad and I said we would do it in person—I think because we both believed it was the least we could do for Lucy. We went into a room and watched them wheel in her body on a gurney.

There she was, my older sister, cold and lifeless. Her beautiful blue eyes stared into space. With a plastic sheet pulled up to her chin, we could only see her face. Dad lifted the sheet and glanced at her body. He left the room.

As for me, I had a strange sensation that this was a seminal point in my life, so I took a few more moments to be with Lucy. I savored every second. I told her that I loved her and that we would take care of her. And I cried.

We claimed Lucy's possessions that were on her when she was killed and arranged for her body to be flown to Boston. We'd have to deal with her apartment later. The airline charged us $500 to fly Lucy to Boston in the cold, unfriendly belly of the plane.

Returning to the police station to talk with the captain and detectives, it was decided they would hold a press conference after Dad and I had left for the airport. We went there in a squad car and, for the first time all day, we took a moment to clear our heads. Suddenly realizing we hadn't eaten all day, we got some dinner, downed it in about a minute, and then found a TV to watch the news. We watched the press conference. Both my father and I were satisfied with the way the police and the DA handled the case. Tired and numb, we boarded our plane and returned to Boston, not comprehending the most difficult days still ahead.

CHAPTER 2

THE HEAVIEST WEEK EVER

OUR FLIGHT BACK TO BOSTON was quiet and uneventful, Dad and I each lost in our own thoughts. When we landed, my cousin picked us up at the airport and told us it had been a busy day at our house. Lots of reporters from the newspapers and television stations hung around to get comments, causing our family members and friends to remain sequestered in the house. Just as my cousin's car headed down the hill toward my parent's house, we saw the last of the TV trucks packing up and leaving. I chuckled, thinking if they'd only waited five more minutes, they would have caught us. That ended our first day of dodging the press.

The next day dawned just as grey and cloudy as the two previous sad days had been. I stayed at my apartment, then went into Boston to be with my parents and to make further arrangements for Lucy's funeral. I felt a tremendous weight on my chest—so many thoughts, memories, and emotions swirling around inside me. I had no idea how to start processing these things. (This is totally normal when dealing with a tragic event; if you're feeling this way too, don't worry.)

Dozens of well-wishers were pouring into the house. It seemed like we had flowers arriving every two or three minutes. Before long, we'd run out of places to put all of them. That's when I called Jane Doe, a non-profit organization that battles domestic violence against women and children. We decided to send this deserving organization any donations we received in Lucy's memory.

I remember the phone call clearly. I called up and said, "Hi, my name is Alexander Sprague. You may have heard about my sister Lucy. Her photo and story appeared on the front page of the paper? We are asking people to please make donations in Lucy's name. What address should we tell them and what special arrangements do we need to have?" After a brief conversation with the director of development, everything was set up. My mother then contacted the newspapers and let them know what we wanted the obituary to say.

The doorbell and the phone wouldn't stop ringing—bouquets being delivered to cheer us, friends arriving to comfort us, and reporters knocking on the door to interview us. We decided that we'd have a news conference at 3:00 p.m. Quite frankly, this was the last thing any of us wanted to do, but we knew that if we gave a statement to reporters, they would leave us alone. Then our family could get on with the difficult tasks that lay ahead. As soon as my sister Cynthia showed up after traveling from Florida, we conducted the news conference.

Each of us made an individual statement at the gathering of about 25 news reporters and camera people. I came out holding a picture of Lucy and me when we were young. My parents commented that her death was an incredible waste, and that they were happy with the job the Chicago police and DA were doing. Actually, my parents and I were nervous about what Cynthia might say, knowing she can get angry and overly passionate. But Cynthia ended up giving the best comment, which turned into the sound bite that the TV and radio stations rebroadcast for weeks. She said, "I find it ironic that Lucy wanted to help the type of person who ended up killing her."

The irony was indeed great.

My friends started to show up shortly after the news conference. I don't really remember them being there, although I do recall my friend Matt coming over. I was talking to him and he went into the other room while I was dealing with something else. Then he said, "Hey, Zander, I have to go." I said, "Why? You just got here." And he replied, "No, Zander, I've been here for three hours."

A blur. And another experience that's normal in these circumstances. I found myself highly focused on what was going on right around me; I had no idea what was happening more than five feet away from me. The rest of the conversations were just noise. I think that's just the way you get, concentrating on only what you have to and ignoring the rest.

It seemed that, every night for a while, friends came over and cooked us a good dinner. In fact, they'd sit around the table most of the evening to keep us company. There seemed to be lots of laughter telling stories of Lucy. I think that's the way it should be, remembering the good while dealing with the bad.

I've observed that people tend to canonize the dead at times like this. I think it's better to remember them as humans who made mistakes—like all of us. We shouldn't be disrespectful of those who died, but remember, they were just like anyone else. Any sibling has both attributes and faults. Telling funny stories about Lucy's attributes and faults somehow lightened the air on those evenings around the table.

As Saturday—the day of Lucy's funeral—came closer, we got busier and busier. We had meetings with the minister who would preside at the service. We had meetings with police officers and close friends of my father's and mother's. They stood by us to give us any help we might need, from food to attorneys in Chicago. Staying busy and taking care of details was tremendously helpful; it kept my mind occupied and away from dwelling on the horrible facts I couldn't change.

This is one of the key elements I'd like you to take away from this book—the need to keep yourself busy. If you spend too much time pondering what's happened, it can swallow you whole like a snake swallows a rabbit. During this time when your emotions are new and raw, try focusing on concrete tasks. Doing activities that have a beginning and an end will help anchor you and give you a sense of accomplishment, however small.

The day of Lucy's funeral arrived. We got ready at my parents' home and drove the short distance to the church. It was hard to tell how many people packed the sanctuary—

somewhere in the neighborhood of 900 people. Cynthia and I led Lucy's coffin out of the church, into the hearse, and numbly went to the upstairs area of the club for Lucy's farewell reception. Our family received about 400 people who expressed their condolences, some standing in line for two-and-a-half hours.

After participating in the receiving line, I had a much better understanding of why it's customary to have one at all. Originally, I had thought that receiving lines were unbelievably sadistic. What could I possibly say to friends and their parents about their loss to make life any better for them? But I found that having people share their condolences was incredibly powerful. In fact, over the past sixteen years we've all commented often about how wonderful we felt soaking in the love surrounding us that day. Now I understand a receiving line's cathartic purpose—providing relief not only for family members in the receiving line, but catharsis for the friends who are grieving, too. On both sides, having a receiving line publicly acknowledges the extreme loss we feel.

The next day, I went with my mom and two aunts to see Lucy one last time at the funeral home. The casket was open and we all said our last goodbyes. We accompanied her in the funeral home hearse to the crematorium—one last ride for Lucy.

After that I simply went home and watched movies. I didn't know what else to do! I felt like I had fallen off the edge of a cliff. One day—surrounded by hoards of people; the next day—no one. In the coming weeks, I had only my girlfriend and my family to lean on for companionship. People didn't call. People didn't stop by to ask how I was. Lucy was gone. My grief wasn't.

I returned to work the next day, again because I didn't know what else to do. I followed my instincts about keeping busy. I needed something to occupy my mind. My father returned to work, too. He also needed something to do. Sitting around the house simply wasn't going to cut it. At my job, I was able to distract myself, however briefly, which I decided was better than doing nothing at all.

I finally put up a sign outside my cubicle that said it was okay to talk to me. I got tired of my coworkers tiptoeing around me. Yes, people would walk by and look at me, but they wouldn't say anything. Nothing they could say would change things. But just chatting with me would have made my world better. I'm a highly social person; I simply wanted people to talk to me first—acknowledge my grief. The worst possible torture I can have is for people not to talk to me.

Outside of work, I'd call my friends and say, "Hi! Let's go do something." Their responses always felt awkward, so I would back off and say, "Don't feel awkward on my behalf. Let me decide when and how I want to grieve about Lucy." What I really wanted to say was, "Don't abandon me. Don't ignore me. Don't pretend it didn't happen. Don't coddle me. Don't make me feel invisible, just because you don't know what to say to me. Don't let me drown in my grief all alone." The truth is, none of us really knew what to say.

On a broad scale, I've learned that most people in our culture don't seem to have any way to talk about death. Their awkwardness shows up as a denial of death. What a belief to carry around—that if we don't acknowledge death, then it does not exist. This misconception may work fine until we're personally confronted by death. When we have to talk to someone who has experienced a loss, we simply don't know what to say. And when we don't know what to say, we tend to not say anything at all.

For me, it was this *not saying anything at all* that was toughest. I wanted to talk to people. I wanted to share my thoughts and feelings. I was curious how others felt, dealing with the loss of Lucy. More than ever, I needed to feel connected, and I did not. Many friends in my circle rallied around me the best they could and I'll always appreciate that—but it was hard for everyone. I didn't always feel connected.

I think feeling disconnected rings true for most people who are deep in grief. We need our friends to be there to simply ask questions and hear the answers. Just sticking around to be present and listen is another key element I want you to take away from reading this book.

As I was riding the bus home after work one day, I was contemplating how I ever survived this horrendous change in my life. I realize this is a common lament by people who have lost someone. They ask, "How will I put the pieces back after they've been shattered into thousands and millions of tiny little pieces? How will I get my life back together?" That's when I came up with the realization that I would survive. This was truly a turning point for me. Until this point, I was simply trying to get through the next hour. I felt like a ping pong ball, bouncing in whatever direction I was hit. Once I realized that I could and would survive, I began to see more light filling my days.

I'm certainly not the first person who ever lost a sibling. I suspect that since you're reading this book, you have lost a beloved sibling, too, and you're feeling really raw about it right now. What I can tell you is—*you will survive.* Of course that seems like easy words coming from someone who has walked further down the path of healing than you. But sixteen years later, I can tell you it is true— *you will survive.*

Knowing that I could learn to deal with my grief and make the best of it—make lemonade from it—was a breakthrough for me. But I also knew I'd have to go fully through the grieving process and feel the intense pain that comes with it.

CHAPTER 3

THE GRIEVING PROCESS

THERE ARE DIFFERENT documented stages of grieving: shock, anger, denial, depression, and acceptance. By January 1997—just a month after Lucy's death—I had already gone through the first stage of shock and was working my way through the anger and denial stages. Depression and acceptance had yet to show up.

Let me talk about each of these stages in the order many people—including me—experience them.

The Shock—A numb feeling that paralyzes all emotions.

The Anger—Yeah! I'm angry. Very angry. How could someone on the cusp of doing great things in her life be taken away? To get over my anger, I had to make the decision that, as unfair as it was, I would probably never understand why Lucy was killed. I wouldn't spin my wheels trying to figure it out. I could spend a lifetime trying to get answers and never succeed. I guess that's a Buddhist-like approach—to be at peace with that decision.

The Denial—Lucy can't actually be dead. I don't *think* this thought nearly as often as I did right after Lucy died, but I still *feel* it. I especially feel it around the beginning of December when the anniversary of Lucy's death comes up. It's hard for me to really imagine that Lucy is gone. The thought is so incredibly final, so complete. What can I possibly do to change that? Nothing.

The Depression—The first month after Lucy died, it was all I could do was to drag myself out of bed and go to work. I remember being so incredibly tired and not knowing why. I was getting plenty of sleep. I'd go to bed at 9:00 at night and get eight, nine, ten hours of sleep. On weekends, I'd sleep longer than I had in a very long time. After a few weeks, I was finally able to drag myself to the gym when the alarm went off in the morning, and I literally mean drag. Going to the gym broke the chain of depression somewhat because, by getting exercise, I pumped up my body's endorphins and felt better. Exercising often helped me feel better. As I regained my energy, I regained my ability to initiate and carry on conversations. In your grieving, I encourage you to make exercise a priority, too. You'll appreciate what it does for you, both physically and mentally.

The Acceptance—Does anyone ever really accept that a brother or sister is gone forever? I don't know; that's a really big question. I accept that an incredibly important chapter of my life—being a brother to Lucy—is over. I accept that I will no longer have the ability to talk to her, ask her opinions. She will never meet my lovely wife or know my daughters— and they will never know her. These thoughts make me sad each and every day. But I also know that things happen and we don't understand why. I may never understand while I live here on this mortal coil. If I can at least accept that I won't know, then I can move on with my life. Perhaps surrendering to the truth of what we can't control helps us gain control. Understanding that is another element I'd like you to take away from this book.

CHAPTER 4

YOU HAVE A CHOICE
TO TAKE CONTROL

I F YOU REMEMBER NOTHING ELSE from this book, remember this: *You have a choice about how you deal with the loss of your sibling.*

I had a choice—and still have a choice now—of how I want to deal with losing Lucy. I feel grateful that my family and I made one specific choice without ever discussing it—that we'd talk about Lucy, we'd remember Lucy, that we wouldn't be scared of remembering her. It's a choice one makes individually, but I'm thankful we all made the same choice.

Every day I remake that choice, and most days, I *do* talk about Lucy. You have similar choices to make. One is to choose complete denial and not even talk about your loss. You probably know people who pull a proverbial blanket over their heads and declare that "nothing is wrong, everything is fine."

But denial comes at a cost. If you do that and let ten years go by, *then* decide to get on with living because you've mourned enough, you can't get those ten years back! In my case, I decided early on that I had my life to lead. Okay, I got busier because of taking care of things for Lucy. But I'm still here. I'm still alive. I don't want to go into mourning and lose my life!

You also have a choice about how you react when people ask, "How you are doing?" Whatever reply you give, you make a decision and empower yourself to take control over what's going on the best you can.

For example, when I went back to my job again after Lucy's death, people I knew well didn't come up and talk to me. Not at all. After the funeral, my friends didn't call me. I felt so alone. So I called them and said, "I want you to call me; I want you to check up on me; I want you to ask how I am. I may tell you that I'm having a really hard time because, God knows, as I go through life, I'll have lots of reminders of Lucy." Since then, I've adopted a motto that I even put at the bottom of all my e-mails for two years after Lucy died. It goes like this:

"When you have a sad memory, be happy you get to remember."

How can you adopt a good attitude about your loss and use it to make lemonade?

Here's what I did. As I would ride the T (the subway) in Boston or walk down the street, I'd encounter little things that reminded me of Lucy. Perhaps it was someone's Opium perfume, perhaps it was a song, or a person's laugh. Sometimes, it was just seeing someone who had the same haircut Lucy did. I'd catch myself saying, "Oh! That's Lucy." Of course it wasn't. But instead of feeling sad, I used every coincidence as an opportunity to be happy that I had this unexpected opportunity to remember my sister. I could hold her image in my heart and shine my light on that wonderful, magnificent life that was my sister.

In a similar way, I suggest that you take control of the process of grieving, the process of talking about your loss if that's what you need. You will have the energy to say, "It's my choice"—whatever your choice might be. If your choice is not to talk about your loss at all, be assured that this option is fine. But also know that talking is ultimately how you will remember. Yes, you may have physical evidence such as clothes, writings, pictures, and more to remind you. But your memories are the strongest, most important things. If you keep the person you love alive and warm and rosy, then he or she lives so much longer on this earth.

How do you deal with your memories and turn them into lemonade? Consider choosing the "cubby hole" method.

Do you remember the cubby hole you had in your first-grade classroom? Perhaps it held your jacket, your painting, your show-and-tell piece, even a toy car or truck. You knew exactly where it was and what you could fit into your cubby hole.

I think we still have cubby holes in our lives. Sometimes, it's really easy to take our memories in and out of our cubby holes. For example, I remember the delight I felt the day

I got my driver's license—that wonderful day that celebrated my newfound freedom. It's easy for me to take that memory out of a certain cubby hole. But as I aged, it got harder to find the right cubby hole for the increasing number of memories in my life.

Hardest of all was finding the appropriate cubby hole for my memories of Lucy. It took me about a year to find the right way to take things in and out, to avoid forcing a square peg into a round hole. But even though it hurt to store my memories in that cubby hole, it wasn't so painful that it took over my life. It was worth doing. And now I know where to find all those memories.

I believe that the more actively you express and store your memories for easy accessibility, the better off you are. I hope you find the right cubby holes for memories of your sibling in the grieving process. It's another element for you to take away from this book.

CHAPTER 5

THE VALUE OF TALK

I REALLY CAN'T STRESS ENOUGH the importance of talking to your friends, family, and even professionals. It can be extremely difficult to talk about a loss. However, in talking about it, you do experience catharsis. Healing happens because you're able to express all those feelings that seemed locked inside.

Some people find comfort talking to a religious leader, be it a priest, a rabbi, a deacon, or a sympathetic friend in your church. Should you decide to attend church services, you may find them helpful as you walk on the path to healing.

I suggest you join a grief group if it feels appropriate. If your loss debilitates you, it may be best to seek professional help from a licensed social worker, a psychologist, or even a psychiatrist.

I would not recommend self-medicating, which means finding solace in alcohol or drugs. Ultimately, you aren't doing yourself any good and it doesn't get you closer to healing. In fact, you could get closer to dying by overindulging in these substances. I can understand feeling that you might be better off if you drink because the pain is so incredible. But remember, you still have a lot of important work to do. At least I know I do, even after sixteen years on my healing journey.

One of the many books given to me after Lucy's death was *Healing After Loss: Daily Meditations For Working Through Grief* by

Martha W. Hickman. It was a wonderfully helpful book. At first, I wasn't sure about its value
among the dozens of books and audios my
family received as well-meaning gifts. Frankly,
some of them weren't my cup of tea. But I picked
up *Healing After Loss* and read it, and read it
again. I would highly recommend it because it
offers short, easily digestible thoughts for each
day. In fact, my mother and I have given more
than sixty copies of this book to friends and
families who've lost wives, husbands, children,
mothers, and fathers. I even gave one to a friend
who lost a bunny.

Finding activities and references that *are*
your cup of tea is important. They're another
form of lemonade along the long, hard path of
healing. Ultimately, that's your goal—to find
appropriate ways to deal with what's missing
in your life and replace that "something" with
new, enjoyable things.

I don't have any miracle sentence in this
book that will make life better for you. And
you surely don't have a miracle sentence that

will make my loss—or someone else's—any better. Yes, understanding that was a powerful revelation for me. No one miracle sentence would get me through my grief. No one thing or one group of things can be said to erase the pain. I simply accept that time heals hearts and allows us to find strength to deal with our loss, to find ways that we can talk (or not talk) about it.

Again, here's what I want you to remember most. As I said earlier, you can make the choice that you don't want to talk about your sibling's death. That's far superior to sitting in silence *waiting* for someone to ask you how you're doing. But whatever you choose, it's important to take control of this decision-making process so you can steer it in the direction you want it to go. For people like me, that action involves talking and sharing the experience of Lucy's death with others. It helps *me* and helps *them* find a way down this dark path of grief and into the light.

CHAPTER 6

SHARING AND CARING

URING A TIME YOU most need support, wouldn't it be like making lemonade if people instantly knew what to say? What if their words would help you find your way through the forest, to once again see the whole forest and not simply the trees right in front of you?

Unfortunately, I have a quite a few friends who have also lost siblings. It was through the strength and love they had for their siblings that they could talk to me about their experiences and feelings. I'd like to share them with you here. May their words help you find a smoother way through the dark forest and into the light.

I'd like to convey their stories in a question/answer format. Please pay attention to the questions, for you may find them effective when asking a friend about losing a beloved sibling.

My thanks to Mary Green, Chad Davis, Brad Smith, Gina Smith, and Alex Baker for candidly answering questions about their losses and sharing them with all of us.

Mary Green

When did you lose your brother?
June 4, 2001.

How old were you?
30 years old.

Where were you when you got the news?
In bed. My brother died early in the morning. My parents were at the hospital with him. They tried calling me repeatedly for a short period of time, but since I was asleep, the message went to voicemail. I was somewhat aware the phone was ringing while I was sleeping, but it didn't register until I was fully awake that it could be an emergency. After the phone stopped ringing, I had a bad feeling and checked my messages. I thought, at the very worst, if it was about my brother, he had taken a turn for the worse with his illness and

had to go back to the hospital. (He was being taken care of at my mom's home with my parents and nurses.) The possibility that he may have died never entered my mind.

Who told you and how?

My dad left the message via voicemail.

What was your first reaction?

Denial. Despair. The feeling that everything was unreal. Crying. Unbearable weight.

What did you start thinking about?

How could this have happened? How can this be true? I don't understand. I thought he'd be okay. He was supposed to be okay. What my parents are going through must be unbearable.

How long was it until you could get to your family?

One to two hours.

What was the funeral like?

It was a memorial service at the Mill Valley Community Center. On Chris's program, which my dad wrote and my friend Maria and I designed on the computer, it said, "Remembrance, a memorial celebration of life." That is the tone our family wished for the memorial. My family had wanted to keep it small and intimate so I did not invite many of my friends. It ended up being bigger than my parents anticipated, which showed an outpouring of love and support for us. My brother had one best friend who worked closely with us putting the service together. In the later years of my brother's life and illness, he did not have many friends, so not many of his peers were there. Most of the people were my parent's friends, as well as other pivotal people and caretakers in my brother's and my lives when we were kids.

However, my brother had a favorite band, MIRV, that he went all over the Bay area to see when he was well enough. Two of the members came to the memorial and spoke. This was really meaningful to all of us because they gave us a glimpse of how my brother was in the outside world as an adult, and how he was seen outside his illness. His disease impaired him and he was self-conscious in his adult life. With that, on top of being a natural introvert, he did not have much of a social life as an adult.

I felt the service was nice and appropriate for Chris. There was catered food and beverages in one room, and in the main room people gathered, sitting or standing in a large circle. Each of us (my mom, my dad, myself) addressed the attendees and talked about my brother. Then we invited anyone else who wanted to come up and say anything they wanted in remembrance, too.

In preparation for the service, we had also gone through the family photos which I then took to Kinko's to get enlarged and they were all over the room, showing different stages of Chris's life. This was important for my mom and dad to have people see different sides of Chris—when he was younger and not sick, and involved in interests he could not pursue later because of his illness. My mom and dad wanted people to know all of Chris, not just the part that had to do with his illness and subsequent death.

The evening before, we had a wake or a viewing at the funeral home that was private. It was almost entirely unbearable, perhaps because it was so real but so unreal. There was my brother, but he wasn't there anymore. That was the hardest experience I've had in my entire life. I have no idea how I got through that. I still can't think about it for long. My mom thought he looked like Prince Charming sleeping peacefully. I felt horrified. He had been embalmed for quite a few days and looked unnatural—because it was unnatural for him to be dead.

How did the receiving line affect you?

The service was too informal for a receiving line. We had a sign-in book at the front and asked everyone to take a rose from the arrangement that had been on top of Chris's casket the evening before. Many people came up to me to express their condolences before we began the service. I was overwhelmed, outside my body, working on automatic for most of the interactions; but not all. I wanted to be gracious, both because I was grateful for the support and also to hold up my end of "hosting" (if that's what you would call it) to take any burden of interaction off my parents, to be strong for my parents, to make sure things ran as smoothly as possible for my parents.

Did you feel numb about your loss?

Yes. I still feel numb at times.

How did people treat you after your sibling's death? How did that make you feel?

People who had gone through losses of their own reached out to me with their hearts and their hands and their experience. Most people acknowledged my loss for which I thanked them and changed the topic of conversation—much, I feel, to their relief as to mine. I didn't want to make them feel uncomfortable and was either struggling hard to maintain as much as possible and continue on with my day or work. At my main job site where people are psychology-minded and knew of my struggle and absences due to my brother's illness, I didn't feel shunned. But I also put on the air of productivity to make everyone (including myself) feel like things were "normal" and I was okay. At the two other job sites where I worked, people were unsure how to treat me, what to say, what questions to ask, or if they were intruding. I ended up writing a general staff letter answering all the questions they were too afraid to ask, acknowledging my brother's death, and explaining some of the grief symptoms I was experiencing that were affecting my work. In that way, I asked for their help in those matters. Symptoms would include forgetting conversations and forgetting to follow through on matters I had agreed to take care of. I asked the staff to please help me by reminding me.

Did you have signs of depression afterwards?

Tons. Due to my work, I am familiar with symptoms of depression and so I understood and recognized them within myself, and accepted them for the most part. The most surprising symptom for me, however, was the unrelenting insomnia I had. For a while, I just went with it and stayed up watching TV every night until my partner got too frustrated with it, and convinced me to get prescription sleeping pills.

Did you cry easily at the thought or mention of your brother's name?

Sometimes I did and at other times I felt totally numb and couldn't talk about Chris or say his name without feeling much. There was no rhyme or reason to which reaction I would have on which day or at which time.

Did you and your family talk about how you were feeling, memories, things that reminded you of your sibling? Do you talk about him now?

Yes, but not all the time. Now we (but mostly my father) reminisce about both the young Chris and the adult Chris as well as what he may have said about a certain current situation. My father still feels a lot of sadness both for the loss and the suffering he (Chris) endured. My mother sees my brother as completing his life's path process, which she would have never guessed would be as it was. But she believes he has successfully completed it.

What is your reaction now when you have reminders of him?

Depending on what I'm doing, I take at least a moment to really remember. Doing that is mostly nice but sometimes bittersweet.

What have you forgotten about him? Do you have things that can help you remember?

Uh, I guess if I forgot, I won't be able to remember to tell you what I've forgotten. Alright. I guess I know what you're asking but truthfully, there are not too many times I choose to remember because it's still so hard. But when I do, in glimpses, the essence of who he is/was is still vivid for me.

What was your relationship with your parents like before your loss? Now?

Sometimes distant or independent. Especially in the last year of my brother's life, they were both consumed with having to take care of him, that required almost all of their energy, time, and focus. I got the message from my parents that it was generally not my responsibility to worry or care for my brother, with some exceptions, but rather to continue leading my own life.

Right after his death, we all became closer as a support for one another, but in general we have all dealt with our grief independently. My mother and father gave some solace to one another, as they both lost a child. But they are divorced and had been for about 17 years at the time of my brother's death.

Do your parents treat you differently now?

Not all that differently. Sometimes, especially my father, is too consumed with his grief. He has apologized for not being able to be there for me. But I reassure him I am okay. My mother, at certain times, redirects the concern and worry she had for my brother onto me now.

How do you feel when you see your parents sad, mad, or in some other way reacting to this loss?
Concerned, helpless.

Have you done any creative projects to remember or in some way comment on how you are feeling about your loss? (i.e., writing, film/video production, music, etc.)
No, my work has been in therapy and with Native American healing traditions.

Did you seek counseling after your loss? Do you feel it helped?
I was already in counseling so I continued.

How long after your loss did you attempt to get back to your normal routine?

Way too soon. Two weeks after my brother's death, which was also just one week after the memorial service. I didn't know what else to do with myself.

What do you do when you have a bad day/week/period?

Depending on my need, I isolate and watch TV, seek the company of my partner or friends, listen to music, go into nature, specifically, spend time at the ocean. Drink wine. I know some of these coping mechanisms are more healthy than others. Sometimes, I need to detach, or go into myself, feel bad, not have to answer to anyone, and wait the period out.

What days/times of the year are hard for you?

Christmas, Chris's birthday, other family times where his absence is very apparent.

Chad Davis

When did you lose your sister?
New Year's Eve, 1977.

How old were you?
I was nine years old.

Where were you when you got the news?
I was actually skiing with William and Frank Baker at Crotchet Mountain in New Hampshire. Mr. Baker did not tell me but he knew. He told me that my folks weren't going to meet me at the Gregg's house, and that he needed to take me home. When I arrived home, my folks met me in the driveway and said that we needed to go for a walk. I remember that I was wearing my ski boots and asked my folks if I could take them off before we went for a walk. The answer was no. That's when they told me.

How did they tell you?

On a walk. They began by describing to me the events leading to my sister's death. They told me about how my sister had woken up asking for orange juice, but that she couldn't keep it down, so they called an ambulance to take her to MGH (the hospital). I think she died during surgery, but I don't recall; it was too many years ago, and too many (or not enough) drugs and alcohol since.

What was your first reaction?

I thought that they were kidding me at first.

What did you start thinking about?

I do remember the first question I asked my folks and have never been able to forget. It is something that I have regretted for the rest of my life. I asked, "Can I have her money?" This statement has haunted me and I am still embarrassed by it to this day.

What was the funeral like?

The only thing that I can recall from the funeral is seeing my dad standing up at the podium in the church giving my sister's eulogy. It was the first and last time that I have ever seen him cry. That hit me hard—to see this strong man who had been my hero reduced to a blubbering pile of crap. I was mad at him for crying.

Did you feel numb about your loss?

No, I missed my sister, but I was not numb. She was my best friend.

How did people treat you after the death? How did that make you feel?

I remember show-and-tell in fourth grade. My family had gone to Maine to my sister's grave and I missed a few days of school. My teacher asked me to share with the class where I had been. When I was about to start telling folks, this little turd named Damien Shea blurted out, "You were burying your sister alive." To this day, if I ever see that punk, he will be terribly sorry, for he might be the one being buried. But for the most part, folks were real nice and compassionate.

Did you cry easily at the thought or mention of your sister's name?

No, I am a man and men aren't supposed to cry, so I don't. But, I don't have a problem with men who do cry. Those men are not afraid to show emotion and suffering, to show what strength of character they have. Maybe someday I'll get there, but I doubt it. If I get a little emotional, I bail so that no one sees me. But I don't cry.

What is your reaction now when you have reminders of her?

I pretend to be indifferent, but we all know better.

What have you forgotten about her?
A lot. I don't know if I want to remember.

What was your relationship with your parents like before your loss? Now?
Good. Great.

Do your parents treat you differently?
No, they still treat me like a child at times.

How do you feel when you see your parents sad, mad, or in some other way reacting to this loss?
I don't see my folks very much, but I don't want to see them hurting. I don't want to see anybody feeling bad.

Have you done any creative projects to remember or comment on how you are feeling about your loss (i.e., writing, film/video production, music, etc.)?
No. My folks do a lot of stuff in my sister's name, mostly educational.

What do you do when you have a bad day/week/ period?

Get stoned. Go shoot.

What days/times of the year are hard for you? Why do you think they are hard?

The holidays. They are hard because we are missing someone in our family and because she died over the holidays.

Brad Smith

When did you lose your brother?
   11 October 1995.

How old were you?
   28 years old.

Where were you when you got the news?
   I had just arrived at work. I am in the Army and was a platoon leader at the time, so my Company Commander told me as soon as I walked in the door that I needed to go see the Battalion Commander. At first, I thought I was in trouble and that I was getting "called onto the carpet" (in trouble). He responded that I wasn't in trouble, but that I had to see him, the Battalion Commander, right away.

   I had just come back from a four-day weekend (Thursday through Monday pass, in essence, an extended weekend). I was in Los Angeles visiting my brother Gene. My mother had called me Thursday night before I left and told me she was getting her gallbladder taken out that Saturday in an operation, but that it would be fairly routine. My uncle (my mother's brother), however, was recovering in the hospital from a mild heart attack. After 30 seconds of pleading with my Company Commander to tell me what the issue was, it suddenly dawned on me—a potential death in the family. I remembered saying to him, "Oh my God, it's my family, isn't it. There's been a death in my family." He could not tell me because he was under strict orders not to (in situations like this, we have to be told by the Battalion Commander), but his face gave it all away that instant. He could barely look me in the face. At that instant, I knew something really bad had happened.

Who told you?

I sprinted out of the office and drove my car ten times above the speed limit to the headquarters building with this virtual Russian Roulette going through my mind. Who was dead? Was it my mom? Was it my uncle? Or could it have been my dad (which I considered a remote possibility)? Was it a traffic accident or something?

When I ran into my commander's office, the Chaplain was there and unfortunately that confirmed my worst fears. My Battalion Commander told me there had been a death in the family and to call home immediately. He broke the brunt of the bad news right up front, but vacated his office, told me to get on the phone, call home, and talk as long as I needed. He said he'd be there with the Chaplain for me when I was done. It fell to Mom to tell me, because she picked up the phone when I called. In no way shape or form did I expect it to be my brother, Gene, whom I'd just seen 24 hours prior.

How did she tell you?

My mother was crying right when she picked up the phone. I thought immediately to myself, "It's not my mom; it must be her brother (my uncle) Colin who's dead due to health reasons." I said, "Mom, get a hold of yourself now. I know this is terrible, but is Uncle Colin dead?" She just cried some more. I said, "Mom out with it! Just say it! Out with the truth!" She said, "No, Brad, your brother Gene is dead. He was killed last night in a car accident."

What was your first reaction?

I was absolutely stunned. It felt like all the blood left my head and arms. I thought it couldn't be true, because I had just seen Gene alive so recently, and before that visit it'd been about nine months since I'd last seen him. I'd even steeled myself for the loss of my uncle or mother on the way up to my boss's office. I thought it was going to be ugly but it was from an avenue of harsh reality that I knew had a rhyme or reason behind it. But Gene's death was like being completely "outflanked" and hit as hard as I could be hit.

What did you start thinking about?

My first thoughts were, "How could this be? I was just out there; there is no way he could be dead." I felt overwhelmed with grief, but at the same time I know I said, "Ok, I am going to make it." And then I knew I had to get home and see my parents—not for myself but the other way around. I knew they would need me.

How long was it until you could get to your family?

I left the next day. October 12th was Gene's 27th birthday, which he was less than 24 hours away from celebrating.

What was the funeral like?

The funeral was cold, somber, and almost unreal. My parents were a wreck, but interestingly united after years of divorce. Gene's death, while it was a horrendous loss to our family in a lot of respects, brought about unanimous common ground to our family, especially to my parents. The divorce was not so nice as I remember it as a kid, but after an event like losing a child, it brought forth a commonality of loss for us all. Ironically, we all had to relate to it and get through it together as a family again.

How did the receiving line affect you?

It felt like putting mustard on a crap sandwich. I wasn't at all happy or excited, but it was weird seeing all sorts of people from the past, especially those folks I hadn't seen in ages. The receiving line was out of respect for our parents, but I hadn't truly grasped the impact of the event yet because I was too busy being strong for my parents. At the time, I just wanted to get out of there and find normalcy. I didn't realize then that it'd be impossible after that kind of an event.

Did you feel numb about your loss? If so, for how long?

Yes, days, maybe weeks. Sometimes, I woke up thinking I'd been dreaming and was relieved, only a split second later regaining the full impact that this ugly real world event was now my reality. I think I was either numb or just being strong for my parents for a couple of months through Christmas and the holidays.

How did people treat you after the death? How did that make you feel?

People in my unit felt sorry for me. They came up and said they were sorry and offered to help. The one thing I really wanted from my boss was not to have all the wives from the wives' group send a plethora of flowers and cards because none of them knew my brother. A simple handshake or card was plenty. I was immersed in enough sorrow and I remember not wanting more.

Did you have signs of depression afterwards?

I don't think so, but then again I'm not the best judge. I know I always thought of Gene at that point as a driving force to be supportive of the rest of my family.

Did you cry easily at the thought or mention of your brother's name?

No. In fact, I was determined not to.

Did you and your family talk about how you were feeling, memories, things that reminded you of your brother? Do you talk about him now?

We talk about him all the time. Not to talk about Gene is (1) not to celebrate his life and acknowledge his life, (2) it is too awkward to suppress and is counterproductive to deliberately forget, and (3) I think remembrance is a form of honor and respect. Now don't get me wrong, I don't think it's healthy to dwell on his death every single day, but it's okay to remember the important things about him.

What is your reaction when you have reminders of him?

It depends, really. Sometimes I laugh because I know he would too. Other times, I feel remorse. One time in Afghanistan, there was a medic his age who was killed in action trying to save his comrades in the Shah e Kot Valley. I thought, damn, that guy was Gene's age when he died. Gene was young and had achieved tremendous success in his short career. It was cut off way, way too short. This kid's life—Jason Cunningham—was cut off way, way too short, also. There's no explaining it. I have friends, lots of friends, who are in harm's way overseas in many places. Hell, I just got back and will be right back out there again shortly. The little I do know is that life is too short even at a hundred years old, so don't waste it. Life is very precious, but I've seen a lot of foreign places and people who don't even remotely think the same way. They feel they've got nothing to live for.

What have you forgotten about him? Do you have things that can help you remember?

Pictures are incredibly important. I just wish I could hear his voice and talk to him again. I miss that the most.

Are you angry about the loss of your brother?

Yes, at times, but it's because I saw his death as being unnecessary. It was due to the utterly preventable negligence and disregard for safety and the law by somebody else. It defined the meaning of vehicular homicide.

Do your parents treat you differently?

Yes and no. They treat me the same as a person, but they really want me to get away from being a front-line-type combatant so they don't have to worry about the loss of another son. I can understand that, but it doesn't stop me from doing my duty.

How do you feel when you see your parents sad, mad, or in some other way reacting to this loss?

I try to understand, but it really depends on the situation.

Have you done any creative projects to remember or in some way comment on how you are feeling about your loss (i.e., writing, film/video production, music, etc.)?

Not in that form. We started a scholarship fund at the Rivers School in Weston, Massachusetts, in Gene's name.

Is there a song that you play when you want to remember your brother?

I think of the Dave Mathews Band's first album because he liked it and it was really popular at the time he died.

Did you seek counseling after your loss?

No, I think my family and friends really helped me pull through during the hard times and I just had to adjust.

How long after your loss did you attempt to get back to your normal routine?

I had to get back to the Army schedule after about three weeks. I didn't really want to, but in the end, it helped me recover. Life does go on, and in a strange way, my training also kicked in. You have to "drive on to the ranger objective though you be the lone survivor."

What do you do when you have a bad day/week/ period?

Usually just be pissy.

What days/times of the year are hard for you? Why do you think they are hard?

I think Gene's birthday is the hardest because he died the day before. In a way, it will always seem as if Gene is in a state of "suspended animation." I will never have pictures of him as an old man or even a middle-aged man. As I get to be in my middle 30s, he'll always be in his middle 20s, in his prime, or cut off just prior. His birthday is a symbol of that melancholy day.

Alex Baker

When did you lose your brother?
March 25th, 2002.

How old were you?
17.

Where were you when you got the news?
In the hallway of the ICU room.

Who told you?
A doctor.

How did he tell you?
Same way the doctors always tell you.

What was your first reaction?
Shock—I didn't move from where I was sitting until someone called at me.

What did you start thinking about?

Everything I tried to think about got short-circuited, so I don't actually remember thinking about anything at all.

How long was it until you could get to your family?

I was with my family at the time.

What was the funeral like?

No funeral—it was a memorial service held at his elementary school. There wasn't a casket present, as we had the body cremated. (You remember, Zander—you were there!)

Did you feel numb about your loss? If so, for how long?

Yes, I don't know that I can point to a specific time that I wasn't "numb" all of a sudden. Going back to school (this was during spring break and I came back on Monday with everybody else) helped, because I got to see other people.

How did people treat you after the death? How did that make you feel?

This surprised me. When I went back to school, lots of people came up to me to say "sorry," even people who probably didn't even know my brother was in the hospital, who had simply heard via word of mouth.

Did you have signs of depression afterwards?

I don't think so, but my friend says I do—still.

Did you cry easily at the thought or mention of your brother's name?

Usually no, but there are a lot of movies that I have a difficult time watching now.

Did you and your family talk about how you were feeling, memories, things that reminded you of your brother? Do you talk about him now?

Yes, but mostly I don't discuss it with my family. For whatever reason, I don't open up emotionally to most people. (I actually recruited a friend to sit with me while I type this.) For the most part, I don't like to bring it up, but I can tell people that, yes, I had a brother who died if it comes up in conversation.

What is your reaction now when you have reminders of him?

This depends. Some reminders don't bother me or are humorous, but if it makes me uncomfortable, I clam up and don't talk.

What have you forgotten about him? Do you have things that can help you remember?

I don't think I know how to answer that.

What was your relationship with your parents like before your loss? Now?

More or less the same…not a whole lot gets spoken about it now. I haven't ever opened up to my parents much at all.

Do your parents treat you differently?

Yes, but I think a large part of that has to do with the fact that I don't live with them anymore.

How do you feel when you see your parents sad, mad, or in some other way reacting to this loss?

Actually this tends to make me rather uncomfortable. I've noticed that I distance myself physically.

Have you done any creative projects to remember or comment on how you are feeling about your loss (i.e., writing, film/video production, music, etc.)?

Yes and no—I haven't written any music specifically for this, but music is a passion that Nick and I shared, so participating in music was simply one way I helped myself deal with it.

Is there a song that you play when you want to remember your brother?

There are songs that remind me: "Blackbird" by the Beatles and "Aqueous Transmission" by Incubus.

Did you seek counseling after your loss?

Counseling wouldn't work for me. I wouldn't say a single thing to the therapist and I'd get nowhere, so I haven't tried it, nor have I any intention of trying it.

How long after your loss did you attempt to get back to your normal routine?

This happened during spring break, and I went back exactly one week later, on the Monday that everybody returned.

What do you do when you have a bad day/week/ period?

Sometimes I call a friend...usually nothing.

What days/times of the year are hard for you? Why do you think they are hard?

This is hard to measure objectively, as it hasn't yet been a full year.

Is there anything else you would like to add?

I have formed associations with things, places, and events, that I somehow relate to Nick's death, and that I now have hesitations approaching. By most regards, I like the city of Portland, but I have no desire to go back—it feels "unclean" to me now.

Gina Smith

When did you lose your brother/sister?
June 26th, 2005

How old were you?
I was 30, he was a few weeks shy of 28.

Where were you when you got the news?
In my home. I'd leapt from bed knowing that something was wrong because the phone was ringing at 6am.

Who told you?
My mom

How did they tell you?
She said, "Josh is gone" and I knew...

What was your first reaction?

Disbelief. I almost fainted and my boy-friend propped me back up.

What did you start thinking about?

When my brother and I had spoken the night before, he had sounded "off". I let it go thinking maybe he had a friend over and didn't want to talk. I thought about calling him back that night. I didn't. I have few regrets in my life, and not calling him back is a HUGE one. Who knows if I could have stopped him from killing himself, but it will haunt me forever I think.

How long was it until you could get to your family?

My parents, my brother and I lived in three different states at the time of his suicide. I was in New York, my parents were in California and we met sometime within the week in Colorado to gather my brother's things. That was the worst flight of my life. Getting off the plane and seeing my parents huddled together, basically holding each other up, was excruciating.

What was the funeral like?

We didn't really have a funeral. We buried my brother's ashes at a spot where we'd camped as a family. It was beautiful and perfect.

How did the receiving line affect you?

n/a

Did you feel numb about your loss? If so, for how long?

I never felt numb about my loss. If anything I began to see things more acutely. Gauging an event's importance through new eyes in a way.

How did people treat you after the death? How did that make you feel?

The reactions varied tremendously. Sibling death holds its own oddities, add in suicide and many people had no idea what to think, say or do. I totally understood, even at the worst times. I remember thinking, "when I get through this and know someone else that suffers loss, I will always remember that saying something is better than nothing". Folks that said nothing at all when I knew that they were aware of my brother's death felt so odd. I have some amazing people in my life, though, and they did some amazing things. Kind gestures that I never would have thought of! For instance my friend Jenn watched my cat while I was in Denver with my parents. She did all of our laundry, put food in the fridge and flowers in the house before we came home...makes me tear up even now!

Did you have signs of depression afterwards?

Oh yes. Fortunately, I'd already put a deposit in on a puppy before losing my brother. The call that she'd been born came three days after my brother died. Having something to prepare for while I waited the eight weeks to take her home was a blessing. After she was home, having to care for her was often my reason for getting out of bed. She was (and still is) very therapeutic.

Did you cry easily at the thought or mention of your brother or sister's name?

Yes, and often. Laughed a lot too, my brother was a funny guy. We still laugh about him...and cry, too.

Did you and your family talk about how you were feeling, memories, things that reminded you of your sibling? Do you talk about him or her now?

My parents were really great about letting it be known that they wanted to hear about him. I felt very open to tell them how I was feeling and share memories of my brother. We still recount funny stories or share how we feel now...all these years later.

What is your reaction now when you have a reminder of him or her?

Mostly a bittersweet memory. I had no idea, though, how sad it would make me when I got married and he wasn't there. Even more so that he'll never know my kids.

What have you forgotten about him or her? Do you have things that can help you remember?

N/A

Are you angry about the loss of your sibling?

Yes. Not all the time, but yes.

What was your relationship with your parents like before your loss? Now?

I had a good relationship with my parents, but it has deepened since losing my brother, especially with my dad.

Do your parents treat you differently?

We were adults when he died, so I don't think they treat me differently, but it would be hard to tell I suppose.

How do you feel when you see your parents sad, mad, or in some other way reacting to this loss?

It makes me sad, sometimes angry with my brother for leaving me to pick up the pieces.

Have you done any creative projects to remember or in some way comment on how you are feeling about your loss? (i.e. writing, film/video production, music etc)

I wrote to my brother a lot after he died. I buried him with a long letter. It felt good to get the feelings out.

Is there a song that you play when you want to remember?

My brother and I both love(d) music. I inherited his CD collection, so I go through that sometimes to reminisce. He called me one time to tell me about a Dixie Chicks song he'd just heard. He said, "I know you probably don't like them because they are kind of country, but they did "Landslide" and it is so cool". I know it sounds nuts, but the number of times that I heard that song after his death was so odd. It was everywhere! And it had been released years earlier. The most amazing time was sitting in a restaurant telling my boyfriend about the above conversation, took a sip of my beer, and the song began to play!! We both smiled and cried.

Did you seek counseling after your loss? Do you feel it helped?

I did go to counseling, and it helped a lot.

How long after your loss, did you attempt to get back to your normal routine?

A few weeks at least. After that I made sure I was in a situation I could get out of if need be.

I worked with kids then too, and they are the best medicine.

What do you do when you have a bad day/ week/period?

If I am having a rough time, I allow myself the space to feel it all, cry if I need to. I tell my kids and husband about what a great guy my brother was, listen to some of our shared musical interests, or watch a movie that made us both crack up.

What days/times of the year are hard for you? Why do you think they are hard?

The last time I saw my brother was on St. Patrick's Day. He had flown out to see me and we went out that night. I almost bailed on him because I was sick, but I went anyway and we had a great time. He died a couple months later and that was it. That night was the last fun night with my brother. The bittersweet memory of that night makes it a rough day.

Any time my family is all together is tough too. Josh was a big family guy and I know that he'd be there if he were still alive. It, still, always feels like something is missing.

If there is anything else you would like to add, please feel free to do so.

CHAPTER 7

SOME PEOPLE
I HAVE HELPED

I'm on a mission to help other sibling survivors. In that role, I've started to coach people going through the loss of a sibling. Now, many of you may have heard about personal coaches, (some people will call it a life coach), I like to call it a personal coach, and it can be a powerful tool for healing. Especially, for sibling survivors, those of us who are finding our grief to be a rather lonely existence.

As stated in the book, a lot of times people don't know how to talk to us or acknowledge our grief, and we feel lonely, and that's why I've started coaching people. I want to help other sibling survivors to define their loss, choose a positive pathway, and fully participate in their life.

I want to take some time and talk about a few of the clients that I've had and helped so that you might find commonality in their experience and find the help that you might need.

Brenda was one of my clients recently. I met her while running in a group, and when I mentioned my book, she said to me that her sister had died 25 years ago and she hadn't really thought about it much. As we continued on our run, we talked about her sister. We talked about her experience of losing her sister, and along the way, I began to talk about Lucy, and she expressed to me that she was ready for some help. I said, "Well, I can do that."

So we started coaching sessions with some phone calls and informal conversations. I listened to what she had to say and heard some of the difficulties that she was experiencing even though it was over 25 years ago, she said she had never really talked about the loss of her sister, and expressed that she was feeling better in being able to talk about it.

During our coaching sessions, we talked about many things, what her sister was like, what it meant to lose her sister, how it affected her relationship with her parents, and about goal setting. The goal setting was important because there were many things that Brenda wanted to do, but, for some reason, just hadn't taken action to do.

One of the big things that she wanted to do since she had taken up running was to run a half marathon. Together we set the goal, figured out a training plan and started down the path to achieve the goal. We also continued our phone conversations. These conversations were sometimes quite difficult for her. I had given her the 28 questions from the end of the book to answer. Answering the questions allowed her to explore her feelings around the loss of her sister and her reactions to it. She found it very cathartic and helpful.

She set her goal to be able to run a half marathon in September of 2012. I am happy to report that she finished that half marathon. Afterwards, I called her and asked her how it went and she said, "You know, it wasn't easy, but it was really great, and I felt that my sister was with me the whole time, and that helped me."

After she finished the half marathon, we had a few more sessions, but she was feeling quite complete and I didn't feel that there was much more that I would be able to help her with at that time.

A work friend introduced me to another client. He knew about my book; his brother had passed away four or five years prior. I started to work with him, and one of the big things that he said was his relationship with his parents had changed dramatically after his older brother had passed away. When he would visit with his parents, the conversations were stilted and awkward. He didn't quite know what to do.

We spent a lot of time talking about that. We talked about what his relationship with his parents was like beforehand and after, and through these conversations, he began to see that his parents' reaction could possibly be that they had lost one son, were afraid of losing another, and were just scared.

I encouraged him to try to have as open and frank conversations as he could with his parents about his feelings of losing his brother and get them, perhaps, to talk about their feelings. These conversations are always difficult. As we mature, our relationship with our parents change, and evolve, so the way in which we talk to each other is different. In some ways, it remains the same. There are certain roles that each person in the family plays, the instigator, perhaps the negotiator, or the peacemaker, but after the loss, relationship dynamics change.

I know personally, I went from being a middle child to technically being the oldest child, and that was something new for me. In all honesty though, I will always think of Lucy as my older sister.

My client knew that his parents couldn't handle going through his brother's personal items and he was having a hard time discussing this with them. His brother was the one who had always taken charge of these things, being the older child. Now, it was left to him. He started to have those tough conversations. It started off a little rough, but he said as time went on it did seem to get better after continuing through coaching. Then, after discussing how it was going, he and his mother and father decided to have a family vacation together. It's something they hadn't done in quite a long time.

They decided to go big and go to South Africa. They went on safari and saw Cape Town, and it was all quite wonderful. He said it was very cathartic for all of them. They laughed a lot, and cried, but he was really embracing the idea that the best way to honor his brother was, in his own words, "To keep him warm in my heart and to remember him."

Shortly after he got back from South Africa, he said he was feeling much better. He felt that a great weight had been lifted. His parents felt better. His relationship was certainly a lot better. They were talking a lot more and they were able to go through some of his brother's personal items, and decide what they wanted to do with it.

It is never easy to decide what to do with the clothes, pictures, furniture, sports equipment etc. that make up someone's life. Disposing of these items feels as if you are disposing of your sibling's life, but you are not. There are creative things you can do to repurpose these items. A coach friend of mine made quilts out of her husband's clothes for her children.

It took my family many years to go through and give away the articles of Lucy's life that we did not want to keep. If it takes you time, that is just fine.

THE
SECOND TIME

I n October of 2007, the first edition of this book was just going to press when my sister-in-law died suddenly at the age of 35. She had a massive cerebral hemorrhage and thankfully did not suffer.

The rest of us, however, were certainly suffering. It was a devastating blow not only for my wife and me, my sister-in-law's family, but most importantly for my brother-in-law.

I again found myself thrusted unexpectedly into losing a sibling. I won't say that my sister-in-law and I were the best of friends but we were certainly close and I consider my in-law's family just like I do my own flesh and blood, and her death was very difficult.

One of the things that was interesting was that I went back and read *Making Lemonade: Choosing a Positive Pathway After the Loss of Your Sibling* because all of the same things that came up when Lucy died were coming up again. I felt just as helpless, just as devastated, just as raw so I went back and I read my book.

I don't mean this to sound self-serving or congratulatory. I didn't know what to do so I picked up my book and I started to read and I found that it helped.

I found that I already had the tools that I needed to figure out how to find the positive pathway, to keep her memory strong and alive. The same way I do to keep Lucy's memory strong and alive.

In the coming weeks and months, I was there to offer support to my brother-in-law as he needed. It's always interesting to see how different people grieve and deal with loss. His was neither right nor wrong; it was just different than mine, and that's fine.

I'm happy to say that he was open to talking with me a little and that he found his own positive pathway and was able to again find love. He is remarried and now has a new son.

I'm so happy to see how he has healed himself and how they keep my sister-in-law's memory alive. His new wife is very understanding about honoring Kelly and keeping her memory alive. There are pictures of my sister-in-law in their house and artifacts from her life. I have great admiration for my new sister-in-law's compassion and understanding.

EPILOGUE

It is quickly approaching the sixteen-year mark of Lucy's death. It seems so surreal that a decade and half has passed. At times, it has been so very hard to even get through the day, and other times the anniversary of Lucy's death comes up and I think "where did this past year just go?" I guess that is how life is; at times we become painfully aware of each minute and other times, unaware of the passing of time. If it is any solace I have found that the journey does get easier and I have found a comfortable place to put Lucy and I cherish her every moment I get.

I would love to hear about your experiences and how you made or are making lemonade. There is a user-generated blog called The Lemonade Stand at

www.makinglemonadebook.com

Feel free to leave a note or e-mail at

zander@zandersprague.com

I hope this book has helped you on your journey.

—Zander Sprague

March 2013

28 QUESTIONS TO MAKE LEMONADE

1. When did you lose your brother/sister?
2. How old were you?
3. Where were you when you got the news?
4. Who told you?
5. How did they tell you?
6. What was your first reaction?
7. What did you start thinking about?
8. How long was it until you could get to your family?

9. What was the funeral like?
10. How did the receiving line affect you?
11. Did you feel numb about your loss? If so, for how long?
12. How did people treat you after the death? How did that make you feel?
13. Did you have signs of depression afterwards?
14. Did you cry easily at the thought or mention of your brother's or sister's name?
15. Did you and your family talk about how you were feeling, memories, things that reminded you of your sibling? Do you talk about him or her now?
16. What is your reaction now when you have reminders of him or her?
17. What have you forgotten about him or her? Do you have things that can help you remember?
18. Are you angry about the loss of your sibling?

19. What was your relationship with your parents like before your loss? Now?
20. Do your parents treat you differently?
21. How do you feel when you see your parents sad, mad, or in some other way reacting to this loss?
22. Have you done any creative projects to remember or in some way comment on how you are feeling about your loss (i.e., writing, film/video production, music, etc.)?
23. Is there a song that you play when you want to remember?
24. Did you seek counseling after your loss? Do you feel it helped?
25. How long after your loss, did you attempt to get back to your normal routine?
26. What do you do when you have a bad day/week/period?
27. What days/times of the year are hard for you? Why do you think they are hard?
28. Is there anything else you would like to add?

CPSIA information can be obtained at www.ICGtesting.com
Printed in the USA
BVOW010112300413

319426BV00006B/87/P

9 780979 503016